THE FIFA WORLD CUP

BY MATT LILLEY

Apex is distributed by North Star Editions:
sales@northstareditions.com | 888-417-0195

Produced for Apex by Red Line Editorial.

Photographs ©: Ulrik Pedersen/NurPhoto/AP Images, cover; Michel Spingler/AP Images, 1, 25; Thanassis Stavrakis/AP Images, 4–5; Shutterstock Images, 6–7, 8, 16–17, 19, 21, 24, 26–27, 29; AP Images, 9, 10–11, 12–13; Mike Kireev/Zuma Press/Newscom, 15; Carlo Fumagalli/AP Images, 22–23

Library of Congress Control Number: 2022912069

ISBN
978-1-63738-291-2 (hardcover)
978-1-63738-327-8 (paperback)
978-1-63738-397-1 (ebook pdf)
978-1-63738-363-6 (hosted ebook)

Printed in the United States of America
Mankato, MN
012023

NOTE TO PARENTS AND EDUCATORS

Apex books are designed to build literacy skills in striving readers. Exciting, high-interest content attracts and holds readers' attention. The text is carefully leveled to allow students to achieve success quickly. Additional features, such as bolded glossary words for difficult terms, help build comprehension.

TABLE OF CONTENTS

CHAPTER 1

THE 2018 WORLD CUP FINAL

t is the 2018 World Cup men's final. France is playing Croatia. The winners will be world champions. Nearly 40 minutes in, the score remains tied 1–1.

Ivan Perišić scores Croatia's first goal during the 2018 World Cup men's final.

Then, France gets a **penalty kick**. A player shoots the ball into the net. France takes the lead.

FAST FACT

The 2018 World Cup final took place in Moscow, Russia.

Croatia's goalkeeper jumps the wrong way to block France's penalty kick.

In the second half, France scores two more times. Croatia cannot respond. In the end, France wins 4–2.

Kylian Mbappé (right) handles the ball during the 2018 World Cup final.

TEEN GOALS

Kylian Mbappé scored France's last goal of the 2018 World Cup. The young star was just 19 years old. He became the second teenager ever to score in a final. Pelé was the first.

Pelé (left) celebrates after Brazil won the 1958 World Cup. The 17-year-old scored two goals in the final.

CHAPTER 2

WORLD CUP HISTORY

The first men's World Cup happened in 1930. It took place in Uruguay. Only 13 teams **competed**. Uruguay and Argentina met in the final. Uruguay won 4–2.

Uruguay scores against Argentina during the 1930 World Cup final.

Spain's goalkeeper makes a save during the 1950 World Cup.

In 1942, World War II (1939–1945) was raging. **FIFA** cancelled the World Cup. The Cup returned in 1950. After that, FIFA held the event every four years.

PLAYER PAY

At first, many World Cup players were amateurs. They didn't get paid to play. So, some couldn't afford to travel. Today, most players are professionals. Many make millions of dollars.

The first FIFA Women's World Cup was in 1991. China **hosted**. The United States beat Norway in the final.

FAST FACT

More than one billion people watched the World Cup final in 2018.

As of 2021, Elena Danilova (left) was the World Cup's youngest scorer. She scored in 2003 at 16. ▶

CHAPTER 3

REACHING THE WORLD CUP

Today, hundreds of countries try to play in the World Cup. FIFA runs the event. The group splits the world into six zones.

Zones are made up of nearby countries. Chile and Brazil are part of the South American zone.

Countries in each zone play one another. The best teams **qualify** for the World Cup.

FAST FACT

Qualifying zone games take place over several years.

In September 2021, Italy played in a qualifying game for the 2023 Women's World Cup.

The World Cup starts with the group stage. The best teams in each group go on to the **knockout stage**. Eventually, only two teams are left. They face off in the final.

BRAZIL ON TOP

Going into 2022, Brazil had played in every World Cup. No other country had done that. With five titles, Brazil also had the most World Cup wins.

In the 2018 men's World Cup, Croatia beat England to advance to the final.

CHAPTER 4

WORLD CUP HIGHLIGHTS

Brazil met Germany in the 2002 World Cup final. Ronaldo played for Brazil. He scored the game's only two goals.

Ronaldo celebrates after winning the 2002 World Cup.

The 2014 World Cup final took place in Rio de Janeiro, Brazil.

The 2014 final was tied 0–0 at the end of **regulation**. But Germany beat Argentina in extra time. Extra time is added when regulation ends in a tie.

THE MOST GOALS

By the end of 2019, Brazil's Marta had scored 17 World Cup goals. She set a new record. Germany's Miroslav Klose held the men's record. He had 16 goals.

Marta (right) jumps for the ball during a 2019 World Cup match against Italy. She scored her 17th goal in that game.

In 2019, the United States played the Netherlands in the final. US players scored twice in the second half. They won their second straight World Cup!

FAST FACT

In 2019, the United States won its fourth Women's World Cup.

FIFA Women's World Cup France 2019™ adidas

Megan Rapinoe (right) won the 2019 Golden Ball. That award goes to the World Cup's best player.

COMPREHENSION QUESTIONS

Write your answers on a separate piece of paper.

1. Write a paragraph that explains the main ideas of Chapter 3.

2. Which country do you want to win the next World Cup? Why?

3. Which country hosted the first men's World Cup?

    A. China

    B. Uruguay

    C. Brazil

4. Which team won the men's World Cup in 2002?

    A. Argentina

    B. Germany

    C. Brazil

5. What does **titles** mean in this book?

With five titles, Brazil also had the most World Cup wins.

    A. names of books
    B. top finishes in events
    C. losses of games

6. What does **amateurs** mean in this book?

At first, many World Cup players were amateurs. They didn't get paid to play.

    A. people who don't earn money for playing sports
    B. people paid for playing sports
    C. people who don't like playing sports

Answer key on page 32.

GLOSSARY

competed
Tried to beat others in a game or event.

FIFA
The group that runs the World Cup. In English, its full name is "International Federation of Association Football."

hosted
Planned an event or provided the space where it happened.

knockout stage
A part of an event in which just one loss removes a team.

penalty kick
A free kick that a player takes against a goalkeeper.

professionals
People who get paid for what they do.

qualify
To make it into a competition.

record
The best or fastest performance of all time.

regulation
The standard 90 minutes of a soccer game.

BOOKS

Abdo, Kenny. *Miracle Moments in Soccer*. Minneapolis: Abdo Publishing, 2022.

Huddleston, Emma. *Legends of Women's Soccer*. Mendota Heights, MN: Press Box Books, 2021.

Morey, Allan. *The World Cup*. Minneapolis: Bellwether Media, 2019.

ONLINE RESOURCES

Visit **www.apexeditions.com** to find links and resources related to this title.

ABOUT THE AUTHOR

Matt Lilley has an MS in scientific and technical writing. The focus of his degree was on medical writing for kids. He loves researching and writing about all sorts of topics. He lives in Minnesota with his family.

INDEX

ANSWER KEY:
1. Answers will vary; 2. Answers will vary; 3. B; 4. C; 5. B; 6. A

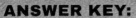